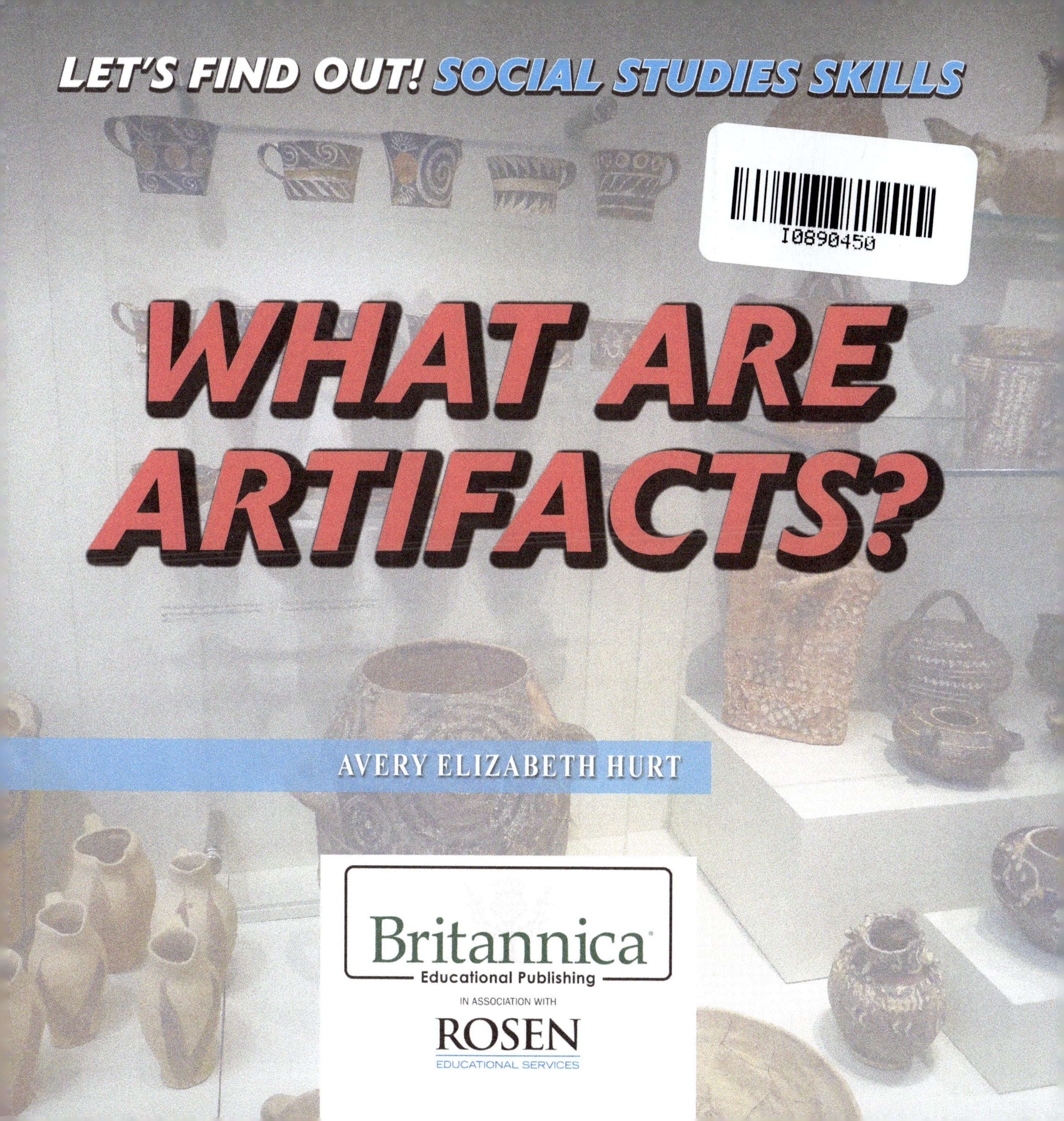

LET'S FIND OUT! SOCIAL STUDIES SKILLS

WHAT ARE ARTIFACTS?

AVERY ELIZABETH HURT

Britannica Educational Publishing
IN ASSOCIATION WITH
ROSEN EDUCATIONAL SERVICES

Published in 2019 by Britannica Educational Publishing (a trademark of Encyclopædia Britannica, Inc.) in association with The Rosen Publishing Group, Inc.
29 East 21st Street, New York, NY 10010

Distributed exclusively by Rosen Publishing.
To see additional Britannica Educational Publishing titles, go to rosenpublishing.com.

First Edition

Britannica Educational Publishing
J.E. Luebering: Executive Director, Core Editorial
Mary Rose McCudden: Editor, Britannica Student Encyclopedia

Rosen Publishing
Jane Katirgis: Editor
Brian Garvey: Series Designer
Ellina Litmanovich: Book Layout
Cindy Reiman: Photography Manager
Nicole DiMella: Photo Researcher

Library of Congress Cataloging-in-Publication Data

Names: Hurt, Avery Elizabeth, author.
Title: What are artifacts? / Avery Elizabeth Hurt.
Description: First edition. | New York : Britannica Educational Publishing, in Association with Rosen Educational Services, 2019. | Series: Let's find out! Social studies skills | Includes bibliographical references and index. | Audience: Grades 1–5.
Identifiers: LCCN 2018014217| ISBN 9781508107026 (library bound) | ISBN 9781508107217 (pbk.) | ISBN 9781508107385 (6 pack)
Subjects: LCSH: Antiquities—Juvenile literature. | Material culture—Juvenile literature. | Archaeology—Juvenile literature.
Classification: LCC CC171 .H87 2019 | DDC 930.1—dc23
LC record available at https://lccn.loc.gov/2018014217

Manufactured in the United States of America

Photo credits: Cover and interior pages background PitK/Shutterstock.com; pp. 4, 5 Courtesy of The Department of Classics, University of Cincinnati; p. 6 Portland Press Herald/Getty Images; p. 7 DEA/L. Balbo/DeAgostini/Getty Images; p. 8 Effi Schweizer; p. 9 Philippe Wojazer/AFP/Getty Images; p. 10 WitR/Shutterstock.com; p. 11 Werner Forman/Universal Images Group/Getty Images; p. 12 AdstockRF; p. 13 Ilia Torlin/Fotolia; p. 14 Justin Sullivan/Getty Images; p. 15 Brendan Smialowski/AFP/GettyImages; p. 16 Mahmoud Zayyat/AFP/Getty Images; p. 17 James King-Holmes/Alamy Stock Photo; p. 18 Eddie Moore/ZUMA Press/Newscom; p. 19 The Israel Museum, Jerusalem, Israel/Bridgeman Images; p. 20 Jeffrey Greenberg/Universal Images Group/Getty Images; p. 21 Courtesy of Annette Rousseau/U.S. National Park Service; p. 22 Mariana Bazo/REUTERS/Newscom; p. 23 Matt Christenson/U.S. Bureau of Land Management; pp. 24, 28 © AP Images; p. 25 Al Seib/Los Angeles Times/Getty Images; p. 26 University of Wyoming Geological Museum, Professor Paul McGrew/Encyclopaedia Britannica, Inc.; p. 27 Daniel Maurer/picture-alliance/dpa/AP Images; p. 29 PHAS/Universal Images Group/Getty Images.

Contents

Look What I Found! 4

Garbage and Graves 6

Big and Little 10

Learning About the Past 12

Not Always Old 14

What's the Date? 16

Tools of the Trade 20

In the Museum 24

Past, Present, and Future 26

All About People 28

Glossary 30

For More Information 31

Index 32

Look What I Found!

It was a rainy day in May 2015. A team of **archaeologists** was working in Greece. They were trying to find clues about the lives of people who lived in that country a long time ago. They had been digging for days without much luck. Then one of them turned over some dirt and saw something green. It was bronze. The team kept digging very carefully. Soon they found weapons, armor, silver

While digging in Greece, a team of researchers from the University of Cincinnati discovers a grave filled with Bronze Age treasures.

and gold cups, beads, and gold rings. These items had been buried for more than three thousand years.

Vocabulary

Archaeologists are scientists who study history by examining what people leave behind.

What these scientists found were artifacts. Artifacts are objects made by humans. Natural objects are artifacts, too, if humans have changed them. Carved bones or knives made from stone are artifacts. Archaeologists study artifacts to learn about how ancient people lived. Artifacts help to solve mysteries about the past.

This sword had been buried for thirty-five centuries before researchers found it.

Garbage and Graves

An Irish coin from 1723, a piece of pipe, a musket ball, part of a comb, and a knee buckle were found at a dig at Fort William Henry in Bristol, Maine.

Archaeologists often find artifacts in garbage pits. It might seem odd to dig in piles of old trash. However, garbage pits are good places to look if you want to learn about people who lived in the past. Garbage shows what people ate and how they lived. Archaeologists found scissors, thimbles, and needles in the garbage of a family who lived in the American colonies

Gold items from the 200s BCE were found in a grave in a mining village in Sudan.

in the 1700s. Those artifacts showed that the family probably made most of their own clothes.

Archaeologists also find artifacts in graves. Buttons and jewelry can last a long time in a grave. Some cultures buried personal belongings with their dead. Archaeologists also find religious artifacts and weapons in graves. All these things give clues about when a person lived and his or her role in society.

Think About It

What do you think an archaeologist could learn from the things in your garbage?

Artifacts might be found anywhere people once lived. Places where cities or buildings used to be often are full of artifacts. So are the ruins of churches and temples. After a very long time, buildings fall down. Over the years, dirt covers the ruins. Archaeologists have to dig through many layers of dirt to find artifacts.

Sometimes people find artifacts by accident. A farmer might uncover an old grave while plowing a field. Someone digging a foundation for a building might discover remains of an older building on the same site.

Ruins of ancient buildings or entire ancient cities have been found under layers of soil.

In France in 1940, some boys explored the hole left by an uprooted tree. They found a cave with images drawn and painted on the walls. The paintings had been made by people who lived twenty thousand years ago.

Prehistoric people painted horned animals, horses, and deer on the walls of caves in France.

Compare and Contrast

If you were an archaeologist, what kinds of artifacts might you find in cities, under existing buildings? What might you find in the fields of the countryside?

Big and Little

Artifacts can be big or little. The pyramids are huge tombs for the royalty of ancient Egypt. The largest pyramid is 481 feet (147 meters) tall. Ancient Egyptians believed they would live in another world after they died. They filled their tombs with things they would need there. Archaeologists have found food, clothing, and even board games in the pyramids. Paintings on the

Ancient Egyptians built these huge stone pyramids as tombs for their rulers.

Compare and Contrast

What could archaeologists learn from studying small artifacts like buckles and buttons? What could they learn from large temples and tombs?

walls show scenes from everyday life. The pyramids and their contents help us to learn about the lives of ancient Egyptians.

In 2016, archaeologists in England found the grave of a man who died sixteen hundred years ago. A belt buckle found beside the skeleton is decorated with images of dolphins and dogs. From this small buckle, archaeologists learned that the man had been a Roman soldier.

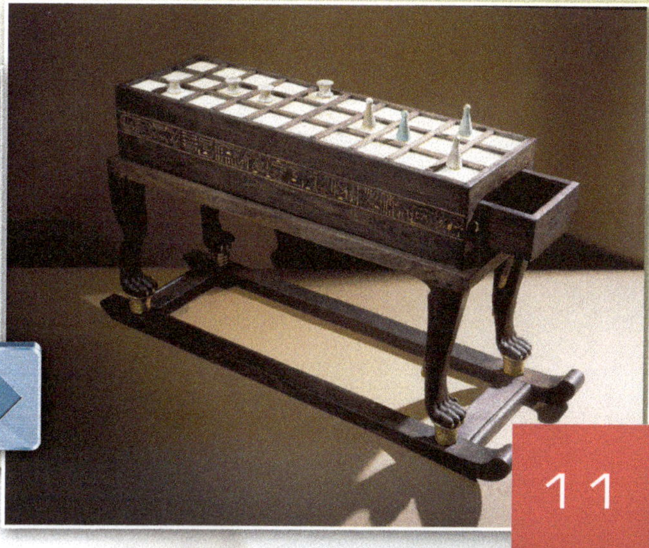

This board game was found in the tomb of Egyptian pharaoh Tutankhamun.

Learning About the Past

It is exciting to see an object that was used by someone a long time ago. But artifacts are more than just objects that look cool. They help us to understand how people lived. Artifacts teach us about the daily lives of ordinary people. We learn what

Prehistoric people in Europe carved daggers from flint, a kind of rock. These knives may have shown the status of their owner.

they ate, what they wore, and what kinds of games they played. We learn the type of work they did and which gods they worshipped.

Artifacts teach us what life was like during the historical periods we study. They help us to understand the history we learn from books, documents, and letters. Artifacts also can give us information not found in books or other writings.

Aboriginal people made these rock paintings in the Flinders Ranges in South Australia.

It is important to learn about people in the past. Their ways of life can help us to understand ourselves better, too.

THINK ABOUT IT

What do your belongings say about you and the way you live?

NOT ALWAYS OLD

When we think of artifacts, we often think of very old things. Stonehenge, a **Neolithic** stone monument, was built more than three thousand years ago. The pyramids in Egypt are more than four thousand years old. Archaeologists found ten-thousand-year-old shoes in Oregon. A boat discovered in England is more than three thousand years old. These artifacts are very old.

But artifacts do not have to be old. The Henry Ford Museum in Dearborn, Michigan, has one of the first

This was the first Apple computer. Computer design has changed a lot since the 1970s.

VOCABULARY

The **Neolithic** period was the later part of the Stone Age, when humans made tools from stone.

A Smithsonian curator works alongside a mask from the Broadway show *The Lion King*.

Apple computers. Steve Wozniak and Steve Jobs built it in 1976. The Smithsonian Museum holds the Simba mask from the musical *The Lion King* and the first Kermit the Frog Muppet. Bill Nye the Science Guy's lab coat is also in the Smithsonian. Even artifacts from the recent past have a lot to teach us.

What's the Date?

Archaeologists need to learn how old artifacts are. The age of an artifact tells them what period of history it belongs to. In some ways, archaeologists are like detectives. They examine artifacts for clues. There are many clues to the age of an artifact.

Archaeologists often use more than one method to

This archaeologist examines artifacts found in an underground room dating back to the Middle Ages.

The white markers on the side of this trench help archaeologists to keep track of the layers as they dig for artifacts.

decide the age of an artifact. Sometimes they look at other objects found nearby. Those objects may tell them when the artifact was made or used.

At other times, archaeologists study the rock layers near the artifact. That scientific work is called stratigraphy. Soil and rock gradually build up in layers over the years. Scientists study when each layer was deposited. How deep an artifact is buried gives a clue about how long it has been there.

Think About It

What are some other clues that might help you guess the date of an artifact?

Neither of those methods is perfect. Sometimes archaeologists need a more dependable way to date artifacts. In those cases, they might use carbon dating.

Carbon dating can date the remains of people, animals, and plants. All living things contain a substance called carbon-14. When they die, this substance slowly decays. Scientists measure the carbon-14 left in the remains of living matter. That amount tells them when the living thing died.

Paper and wood contain carbon because they are made from plants. Carbon dating was used to date the Dead Sea Scrolls, ancient texts

Two scientists adjust a machine used for carbon dating artifacts.

This bit of the Dead Sea Scrolls was found in 1947. Carbon dating shows the scrolls to be more than two thousand years old.

found in the Middle East. Many artifacts do not contain carbon, but they might have bits of organic material on them. For example, a sword might have traces of blood. By dating the blood, archaeologists can tell how old the sword is.

Like other methods, carbon dating is not perfect. It is not accurate on artifacts more than about fifty thousand years old.

Compare and Contrast

Which dating methods could you use for artifacts made of stone or metal? Which methods could you use for artifacts made of plant fibers or bones?

Tools of the Trade

A site where artifacts are found is often called a dig. But archaeologists do not just shovel piles of dirt. They are very careful. It takes many years of training to do their work properly. Before they start digging, they prepare the site. They divide the site into **grids**. That way, when they find something, they know exactly which part of the site it came from. They

These archaeologists, digging at a site in South Africa, are careful to mark the site with a grid.

take photographs of the site. They also make lots of notes.

Archaeologists do not use big shovels. They use small trowels and penknives. They do not want to miss small artifacts. Even if they discover something big, like a buried wall or building, they are very careful not to damage it. Finding artifacts is very exciting. It also takes a lot of patience.

VOCABULARY

Grids are a series of squares or rectangles that help people to locate things on a map or other surface.

Archaeologists' tools can be surprisingly small and delicate.

Compare and Contrast

How would an archaeologist working fifty years ago have explored the remains of an ancient city? How would a modern archaeologist explore similar remains?

Here, a scientist flies a drone over an archaeological site in Peru.

A long time ago, archaeologists did most of their work by hand. Today they have high-tech tools for finding and recovering artifacts. Satellite imagery programs like Google Earth can help archaeologists find remote sites. Drones can photograph sites

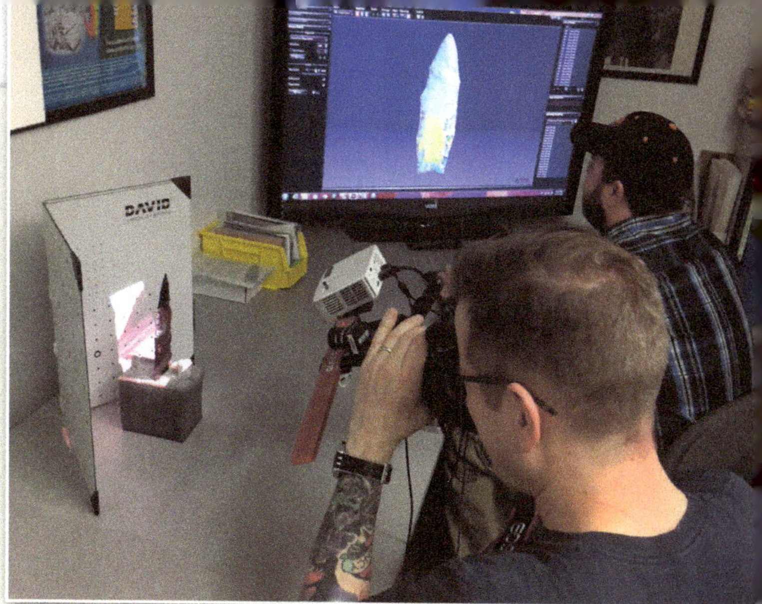

After scanning an ancient spear point into a computer, researchers can use a 3D printer to make a replica of the spear.

from the air. X-rays make it possible to examine artifacts without disturbing them. Some archaeologists have used a robotic snake. The snake has explored caves dug by ancient Egyptians.

Archaeologists collect a lot of data about sites and artifacts. Modern computer programs help to sort that data. Some computer programs make virtual representations of sites. Archaeologists use these representations to study the site. Virtual sites also can be used to teach people about archaeology.

Archaeologists still use maps and trowels and brushes. But new high-tech tools make their jobs easier.

In the Museum

Archaeologists must be very careful with the artifacts they find. Exposure to light and air can harm artifacts. A piece of cloth might last thousands of years in a dry tomb. However, it could quickly rot when exposed to damp air. Archaeologists look carefully at the conditions of the site where they find an artifact. Then they try to make as few changes as possible when they move it. Sometimes artifacts

A special vault in the US Holocaust Memorial Museum keeps artifacts in good condition.

These baskets at the former Southwest Museum in Los Angeles, California, are sturdy enough to be handled by a museum curator.

are treated with chemicals to help preserve them.

After artifacts are collected, they usually are stored in museums. Museums have special rooms and cabinets for protecting artifacts. Museums may allow visitors to touch some artifacts. Other artifacts are kept in special cases to protect them.

THINK ABOUT IT

How does it make you feel to look at an object that was used long ago?

Past, Present, and Future

Throughout history, people have built many societies and civilizations. Those societies changed and sometimes collapsed. Past societies faced many of the same problems we do. They had wars and peace. They had times of plenty and times of famine. By studying artifacts, we learn how people in the past faced those problems. That knowledge can help us to make better choices about our own future.

Digging for artifacts can be hot and dirty, but it is important work. It helps us to learn about past peoples.

VOCABULARY

A **prediction** is an idea about what will happen in the future.

Today we are experiencing climate change. The climate has changed many times before. People in the past had to cope with ice ages, droughts, and floods. Artifacts show us how they managed. We can learn about the kinds of houses they built and the foods they grew when their climate was changing. Artifacts teach us how they built dams and stored rainwater. Studying the past can help us to make a **prediction** about the solutions we try now.

This ivory figure, found in Germany, dates to a prehistoric ice age.

ALL ABOUT PEOPLE

These archaeology students sift dirt for early American artifacts from the Raleigh Tavern in Williamsburg, Virginia.

Studying the way people lived in the past helps us to understand the past. It helps us to make better choices about the future. It also helps us in the present. Past cultures were very different from cultures today. But we still can find similarities between past ways of life and the ways people live now. Learning about past cultures can help us to

These flint daggers, now in the National Museum of Denmark, are from the period 2000–1500 BCE.

understand different cultures in our world today.

Archaeologists work all over the world. They use many techniques and tools to find and preserve artifacts. They study human-made objects from the Stone Age to today. They study clothing and cathedrals, tools and temples, graveyards and garbage. Artifacts are objects that people made and used. When we study artifacts, we learn about people, not just things.

Think About It

What artifacts of our time do you think future school groups will look at in museums?

Glossary

ancient Very old; more than about fifteen hundred years ago.

bronze A type of metal made by combining copper and tin.

culture The characteristic features of everyday life shared by people in a particular place or time.

data Information that is used in calculating, reasoning, or planning.

decay To lose strength; to break down.

deposit To lay down, place, or put.

document A written or printed paper containing information, usually legal or official information.

exposure The state of being uncovered or unprotected.

famine An extreme shortage of food.

museum A building or part of a building in which objects of lasting interest or value are displayed.

organic Having to do with living things.

preserve To keep, or to save from loss or ruin.

remains Whatever is left over or left behind.

royalty Kings, queens, and other members of a royal family.

ruin The remains of a building or town that has been destroyed or has decayed over time.

site A place where a town, building, or event is or was located.

society The system of community life in which individuals live.

temple A building where people worship.

tomb A house or burial chamber for dead people.

trowel A small hand tool with a curved blade, often used by gardeners.

virtual Occurring or existing primarily online.

For More Information

Books

Hoobler, Dorothy, and Thomas Hoobler. *Where Are the Great Pyramids?* New York, NY: Grosset and Dunlap, 2015.

Kelley, True. *Where Is Stonehenge?* New York, NY: Grosset and Dunlap, 2016.

Panchyk, Richard. *Archaeology for Kids: Uncovering the Mysteries of Our Past.* Chicago, IL: Chicago Review Press, 2001.

Romero, Libby. *Vikings.* Washington, DC: National Geographic Kids, 2018.

Wood, Alix. *Uncovering the Culture of Ancient Greece.* New York, NY: Rosen, 2016.

Websites

Children's University of Manchester: Explore Ancient Greece
http://www.childrensuniversity.manchester.ac.uk/learning-activities/history/ancient-greece/explore-ancient-greece

Mocomi: The Aztec Civilization
http://mocomi.com/the-aztec-civilization

National Park Service: Archeology for Kids
https://www.nps.gov/history/archeology/public/kids/index.htm

Index

ancient Egypt, 10–11, 23
archaeologist, 5
artifact dating, 16–19
artifact preservation, 25, 29

carbon dating, 18–19
carbon–14, 18
cave drawings, 9
climate change, 27

Dead Sea Scrolls, 18–19
decay, 18
digs and discoveries, 6–8, 10–11, 14
dig site, 20–21
drones, 22

England, 11, 14
exposure (light and air), 24

garbage pits, 6
Google Earth, 22
graves, 7, 8, 11
Greece, 4

Henry Ford Museum, 14
history, understanding of, 12–13, 26–27

Jobs, Steve, 15

museums, 14–15, 24–25

Neolithic, 14, 15

pyramids, 10–11, 14

Roman soldier, 11
ruins, 8

satellite imagery, 22
Smithsonian Museum, 15
Stone Age, 15, 29
Stonehenge, 14
stratigraphy, 17

temples, 8, 11, 29
tombs, 10–11
tools, 20–23, 29

virtual sites, 23

X-rays, 23